When
Not Yet
Is
Now

COLOSSEUM BOOKS

James Matthew Wilson,
series editor

When Not Yet Is Now

Samuel Hazo

Franciscan University Press

Franciscan University Press
1235 University Boulevard
Steubenville, OH 43952
740-283-3771

Distributed by:
The Catholic University of America Press
c/o HFS
P.O. Box 50370
Baltimore, MD 21211
800-537-5487

Photograph on page 104 by Roy Engelbrecht
Printed in the United States of America.

Library of Congress Cataloging-in-Publication Data
Names: Hazo, Samuel, 1928– author.
Title: When not yet is now / Samuel Hazo.
Description: Steubenville, OH : Franciscan University Press, [2019]
Identifiers: LCCN 2018053023 | ISBN 9780999513453
Subjects: LCSH: American poetry—21st century.
Classification: LCC PS3515.A9877 A6 2019 | DDC 811/.54—dc23
LC record available at https://lccn.loc.gov/2018053023

Mary Anne's

Contents

When
Not Yet
Is
Now

When Not Yet Is Now

A week of April Fahrenheit
   in late February or March
   is all a crocus needs
   to sprout and bud.
                  The last
   defiance it can mount
   against a likely frost
   is brazenly to blossom.
Waiting to bloom until
   it's safe to bloom is not
   for crocuses.
               They have
   the courageous impatience
   to bloom, though many call it
   folly, whenever they're ready.
If they live, they live as crocuses.
If not, they die as crocuses.

I
Surrounded
by Space

Remembering My Father Remembering

He never recovered.
                     Passing
the cemetery, he looked away.
Often he listened alone
   to recordings of classical poems
   of heartbreak sung in Arabic.
Lament as art both saddened
   and soothed him.
                    One night
in the Adirondacks, we drove
together to a mountain cove
and parked.
                Surrounded by space
and stars, we sat, listened
and said nothing.
                Later
I realized he must have come
there once with my mother
and wanted only to relive
and share that memory with just
the two—the three—of us.

Lost Son Found

Conceived but unborn, he lasted
   for three months.
                          He would
   have had my name, and I
   some alternate.
                        Had he lived,
   I'd be the middle son
   between my brother and him.
What difference does it make?
A life is a life, and years
   are the least of life's assurances.
I learned of him by chance
   from an entry in a notebook
   my mother kept in the twenties.
"Had miscarriage in Rochester."
Knowing that I lost him
   as a brother changes how
   I see myself.
                    It shatters
   what used to be the past.
Other entries in the notebook
   span from nineteen sixteen
   onward.
                "Heard President
   Wilson in Oakland."
                       "Imagination
   is love with poetic fervor
   and peculiarly private as it is
   sacred."
               "Both Sam and I are
   perfectly happy."

                    "Sang
        in Detroit and was applauded."
Of the lost boy there's not
        another word.
                        After my mother
        had me and my brother,
        did she see him in us?
I'll never know and never
        had a chance to ask.
She died at thirty-five.

Life as a Vow

She'd made a deathbed promise
   to our mother to raise the two
   of us.
            She never broke it.
Not for marriage, money,
   or other options ...
                    Later,
   when my brother and I were
   off to college or in the service,
   she lived alone for seven
   years, trolleying to work
   and back, grocering en route
   and cooking for herself
   by herself.
            For fifty-seven
   months she worked and lived
   like that so we would know
   that home was there and waiting.
That's called devotion.
                    Otherwise,
   she judged a woman by how
   she dressed and carried herself
   in public.
            Once at a funeral home,
   a woman in a black dress
   and black hose asked her, "Katherine,
   how old are you now?"
                    Without
   a pause she answered, "Ninety-seven."
The woman gasped, "Katherine,
   you don't look it!"

After
we left, I asked her, "Why
did you say you were ninety-seven
when you're really sixty?"

"She
wanted me to be ninety-seven."
Of all women, the only ones
she admired were our mother
and her sister-in-law.

"It takes
a good woman to live
with my brother."

Among
my memories, the one that lasts
is the morning I left for Parris
Island.

We waited for our trolleys
together.

Mine came first.
We kissed.

After I boarded,
I looked back and saw her standing
so alone, so utterly alone.

The Less Said, the Truer

Love comes to men through the eye; to women,
through the ear.

—ARAB PROVERB

When Cyrano proclaimed his passion
   for Roxanne, he spoke from the shadows.
Seated on her balcony, she never
   even saw the man but loved
   what she heard.
                    There's more
   to this than mere romance.
All those who say that love
   is based on age, height,
   religion, status, wealth, or race
   are talking mergers, not marriage.
The man a thoughtful woman
   allows to enter her body
   needs more than these to qualify.
It's what she hears or sees
   in his eyes that matters to her.
For lack of an alternative,
   call it the language of the heart ...
Bill's wife-to-be spoke only
   Japanese.
                He felt what she meant,
   and their thirty years together
   prove it.
             Taller than Faisal
   by half a foot, Nouha
   left Syria to marry him
   because she liked "the look
   in his eye."

When Anne met
Pamela's French fiancé,
she told her, "I'd marry him
if I had to live in a sewer."
Although her mother disapproved,
Rebecca explained, "I'm not
marrying my mother."
Twenty
happy anniversaries later,
she pleaded with friends, "Please
be nice to my mother."
What else
but love explains why Trish
mounted a Harley-Davidson
with Mark, who steered it
after midnight through the rain
from Pittsburgh to Washington
with just one stop?
In order
to prevail, love challenges risk.
Deny that at your peril.

Always Once Again

No benefit gives pleasure unless it is enjoyed in company.

—ERASMUS

I've long since put aside
    the lures of wealth and health
    and other delusions.
                    I think
    of travel as a myth for those
    obsessed with mileage.
                   Emily
    Dickinson journeyed everywhere
    by word but rarely left her home
    or room in Amherst, Massachusetts.
Ribbons clustered in rows
    on military tunics show
    where the ordered bearers
    served and survived.
                  They
    age in lockstep into history
    that buries everything but love.
Dressed alike for sleep
    or unalike for deeds, we opt
    in flux for love until
    our nights and days depart
    like afterthoughts …
              But Anne's
    hibiscus keep their own time
    by flowering in full from dawn
    to midnight and beyond.

  Jenny

        and her infant daughters say
        there's nothing more to want.
Kyle's love for Murray grows
        dearer as the end draws near.
While giving death its due,
        no appetite can rival for intensity
        the sacred pact of lovers
        in the very act to gratify
        as they are gratified.

                                And then?

While equally pleased and eased
        and assured of sequels, they part.

Wedding Night

They kiss like intimate strangers.
Their bodies bridge the differences
    that make them more than
    who they were.
                Becoming two
    as one is what they've chosen.
Or has it chosen them?
It's certainly expected to impose
    some getting used to.
                 They speak
    the silent alphabet of touch
    that makes the world's finalities
    less daunting than they seem.
Another life has suddenly begun.

Mystery Has No Name

It's surfacing from farther down
    but slowly—so slowly that
    it seems no longer rising
    but stalled.
              It's like the magic
of sleep when dreams assemble
on their own until they're whole.
Or when a rose becomes
    a rose from bud to blossom
    overnight.
              Or how a photograph—
developing—becomes itself
in glossy black and white
before our eyes.
              Where are
the words that say that life's
what's brought to light not *by*
but *through* us?
              If we
are praised for that, it's more
than we deserve.
              This may
explain why Michelangelo signed
none of his sculptures but
the *Pieta*.
              He did that only
as an afterthought to show
that he, not Gobbo Solari
of Milan, had made it.
              Michel
Angelus Bonoratus Florent
Faciebat appears on the sash
of the Virgin.

                    Carved in marble
            from Carrara, that made the *Pieta*
            less tributary to the grief
            of Christ's mother than openly
            the work of no one else
            but Michelangelo!
                                    Of Florence!
            Later he regretted having done it
                and blamed it all on vanity.
            By then it was too late.

II
The Remaining
Two-Thirds

Imagine That

To know is nothing; to imagine is everything.

—ANATOLE FRANCE

Living as I do, not far
  from franchise housing for retired
  seniors, I'm bored by the sameness
  of it all.
            The houses duplicate
each other to the last brick.
I call it pre-cemetery living.
Somehow this seems to be
  our common DNA.
                    Soldiers
  in similar platoons rehearse
  with similar arms for similar
  wars.
            Similar skyscrapers
  dominate similar cities.
Once known as overalls, denims
  are the slacks of choice that make
  all students similar as twins.
Some choose to slit them at the knees
  or buy dissimilar brands
  of similar slacks that come pre-slit.
Everything seems scripted
  for sameness to mock the threat
  of difference.
                    Compared to what's
  next door to me, they're all
  facsimiles ...
                    Using rocks and stones
  the prior owner left,

.

my neighbor built a wall
man-high beside his driveway.
He mortared stone on stone
like puzzle pieces in a once
and perfect fit ...
                              Trusting
in abeyance, Roebling
suspended steel in space
from Brooklyn to Manhattan.
And Shakespeare mortared words
together into thirty-seven
plays where everyone
stays "once and only" forever.
As for another Brooklyn Bridge
or *Hamlet*?
                         Neither Roebling
nor Shakespeare could manage that.

The World We're Here to Make

My body's eyes are fingertips.
They let me see whatever
   I touch: a waxed tabletop,
   an apple in my palm expecting
   to be bitten, my wife's eyelids
   parting when I kissed her awake.
And words remember themselves
   like felt thoughts or vows ...
Because returning from Cairo
   was impossible, my student said,
   "I see you never."
                       Bouncing
   a ball on the porch, a boy
   smiled and said, "Look,
   I'm making my ball happy."
But why go on?
                 What touches us
   keeps living on without
   our willing it because it's felt.
We're much like lovers who long
   to touch and hold, since then
   they feel what touching lets
   them feel.
                Their feelings live
   again as poetry, paintings,
   or music.
             Detractors say
   creators are mere copyists
   since God alone can make
   something out of nothing.
Frankly, they miss the mystery.
Because both Testaments reveal
   we're made in God's likeness,

we reimagine what we feel
in words, colors, or sounds.
That's more than copying.

It's
re-creating what would otherwise
be lost.

We're egotists enough
to try.

Sometimes we succeed.

Down to Earth

At sea level we can live without
   assistance.
                  Invading lethal
oceans or the stratosphere
as divers or astronauts, we take
sea level's assets with us
to survive.
             What does it prove
beyond the obvious?
                  Challenge
and adventure have their place,
but how can they compare
with life or gratitude or poetry?
Or love?
            "Earth's the right place
for love," wrote Robert Frost,
"I don't know where it's likely
to go better."
             Although
we've made a menace of the world
and clogged the seas and space
with navies and satellites, I side
with Frost.
            What makes us
mock ourselves by mechanizing
everything?
            I ask Crystal,
"Would you rather receive a love
letter handwritten or emailed?"
She answers by writing her name
in full with a fountain pen
as if she were signing a poem.
When I inquire about the six
rings she's wearing, she's just
as personal.

One ring is her
birthstone; the next,
her grandmother's; the third,
her graduation ring; the fourth,
because she is part-Irish;
the fifth, her wedding ring;
and the sixth, a gold dolphin
that almost seems to be smiling.

Unbudgably Yours

Summering in Pennsylvania
  and wintering in Florida
  would give me two addresses.
I've long since settled for one
  and call it home.
              I shovel
  my way through driveway snow,
  unbox a hat I hate
  to wear, and struggle into gloves
  I should have thrown away
  five years ago.
              I know
  that trees are slumbering in place.
  that grass stays hidden under lawns
  of snow, that roots and bulbs
  await a warmer reveille.
I let the chillier mornings
  help me reach the resurrection
  of a greener life when I can
  waken to enjoy the pleasure
  I deserve for earning April.

Enigma

Happiness is by nature inexpressible.

—OCTAVIO PAZ

We try but fail to say
    exactly how it feels to return
    home after miles, after years.
Surviving sleep, we realize
    we never plunged unparachuted
    down the sky or walked barefooted
    over broken glass or hot coals.
We breathe relieved and then resume
    living the remaining two-
    thirds of the day or the life
    that's left.
            To write or speak
    the words for happiness or gratitude
    assumes that we have mastered
    a tongue without grammar
    or syntax.
            Our efforts end
    in silence or embarrassment
    or both.
            What does it prove
    except that happiness is known
    only through happiness itself?
Reduced to words, it vanishes.

BC and AD

Since yeast reminds them of death,
   the Jews eat bread unleavened.
For them there is no afterlife—
   just *life* menaced by death.
Beyond and after lamentation,
   Jews pray to live on only
   in their children or Jewry itself.
Not quite reincarnation but more
   than memory . . .
                   Orthodox Christians
   worship the risen Christ and leave
   Gethsemane and Golgotha to history.
Catholics do just the opposite.
Nailed and lanced, their Christ
   reveals on cross after cross
   the agony of crucifixion.
                   Protestants
   revere Christ but nix the papacy.
Who else but God would tolerate
   such variations in belief unless
   it helped belief itself to live
   long after it was dogmatized
   to death?
             It's living still
   exactly as a song keeps
   singing when the song is done,
   a dance keeps dancing when
   the dance is over, and a poem
   lives in its entirety only
   at the moment when it ends.

Suspended Sentence

A clean slice through the neck
   of a rooster separates the rooster's
   head from its body.
                      Beheaded,
   the body runs in circles,
   flapping its wings until
   it realizes that it's dead
   already and dies for good.
Between the first and final
   death?
            Suspense.
                  Ted
   at ninety-five was asked
   how being ninety-five felt.
"I died ten years ago,"
   he said, "ask somebody else."
Told he had three months to live,
   Bronco demanded, "Which three?"
When one comic turned a hundred
   on his sick bed and was asked
   what words he wanted spoken
   at his funeral, he answered,
   "Surprise me."
              Other epitaphs
   survive, but none can match
   the secrecy of Lazarus.
                 Apart
   from Christ, no one but Lazarus
   died and returned, and Lazarus
   alone was doomed to face
   death twice.

The rooster in him
should have balked at such
a fate unless he'd glimpsed
some preview of an afterlife
between Deaths One and Two
that silenced all his doubts.
Why did he keep that to himself?

III
Posthumous
Fame

Jerzy Kosinski

I heard the news while driving
   and pulled off the highway.
                        How
   could a man so gifted exit
   in a death by choice?
                Here
   was someone who could stand
   at attention in deep water,
   inhale and exhale softly
   and not sink while never
   moving.
             Creating a general's
   uniform he designed himself,
   then wore to prove the power
   of uniforms, he gained entrance
   wherever he went.
              By chance,
   he missed the flight from Paris
   to California to attend the party
   where Manson murdered everyone.
He played polo by day
   and accompanied vice squads
   on drug raids after midnight
   in Manhattan.
            Warren Beatty
   and Peter Sellers were friends,
   but so were cab drivers,
   poets, and bellhops.
             Despite
   accusations of plagiarism
   and the rest, I found him
   totally original.
            I see him still
   that way—trustworthy and ready

with a new story that's better
than the last one, embarrassed
by praise and always prone
to understatement.
                    I wrote that
in condolence to his wife.
                    Regarding
his detractors, I should have written
that disparagement is envy's tribute
to talent.
          Kiki's answer
was a single sentence, "Your letter
was a bridge to the rest of my life."

Lifers

Life is what it makes of you when ill,
and what you make of it when well.

Jeanne Louise Calment
   celebrated one hundred
   and twenty-two birthdays.
For those who measure life
   by numbered years, Madame
   Calment's the empress of longevity.
Madame Calment herself
   downplayed her birthdays,
   gorged on chocolate, rode
   a bicycle, and smoked.
                 As a girl,
   she knew Van Gogh in Arles.
She sold him paints.
             She found him
   "dirty," "disagreeable," and "ugly."
I'm half impressed.
            Is outliving
   friends and family something
   to celebrate?
           Is it a blessing
   or a curse to reach an age
   where you have trouble recognizing
   anyone, including yourself?
Barring diseases, crime,
   accidents, or war, our average
   span is fifty years shorter
   than Madame Calment's.
             If life's
   worth living only when shared,

how many of her years
were shared?

        With whom?

           How long?

If she lived only by
and for herself, what difference
does it make if she survived
for more than a century?

        Not
that survival is ignorable.

        It
mattered enough for Tithonus
to pray that he would live
forever.

      After the gods
consented, he learned the hard way
that living on's not everything.
His skin wrinkled, and his eyes
clouded.

      Finally, he babbled
like a two-year-old, and forever
became a synonym for hell.
If that's the gift a long life
offers, who needs it?

      Living
for someone else or saying
something unexpected but
true seems worthier by far.

Once Removed

To see how posthumous fame
    defaults into celebrity and profit,
    travel to Arles.
                The name
and profile of Vincent van Gogh
abounds on posters, T-shirts,
coffee mugs, appointment
calendars, and coins.
                His paintings
are everywhere but only
as reproductions.
             Not one original
exists in Arles or anywhere
in all Provençe.
            The Cloister
at St. Remy where he
was cared for is closed
to visitors.
           His likeness in bronze
as sculpted by Zadkine was stolen.
Its photograph is posted in the Cloister
beside Zadkine's curse
upon the thieves.
            In Arles,
Van Gogh, who sold but
one painting in his life,
lives on as hearsay and merchandise.
Such ironies are not confined
to France.
          God knows, we've done
no better with Jesus bumper
stickers, Mark Twain ballpoints,
Hemingway cigars, and Gettysburg
water bottles for sale

on paid tours of the battlefields
that gave us the rare exception.
Lincoln's address was so brief
that it was over while people
were still being seated.

                                  Somehow
his two hundred and seventy-two words,
billed simply as "Remarks by the President,"
outlived the moment on their own.

Galeano

You earned what all great writers
   earn: derision, envy,
   prison, exile, hatred,
   and immortality.
              For courage
on a page, no one comes close
to you.
          Who else has shown
the world its "open veins?"
And who but you could call
   Neruda, Otero, and Alastair
   Reid his friends?
            I often
wish my Spanish were good
enough to read your books
in Spanish and see *exactamente*
what's lost in translation.
              First among
your enemies were slave owners,
killers, and torturers.
           While some
considered the body a sin,
a machine, or a business, you called
the body a fiesta.
          Soccer
alone deserved a book
from you and got it.
          Balding,
you sought a cure, found none,

and lived thereafter boldly bald.
There's no replacing you.

                                Exiled
for years in Spain, you waited
for Uruguay to change.

                                Braulio
Lopez, a guitarist in Montevideo
who sang the anthems of rebellion,
had his fingers crushed in prison.
Deported, he shunned all talk
of his imprisonment when you
contacted him in Barcelona:
"My hands will heal, I'll play
and sing again, and I don't
want to doubt the applause."
Eduardo, even you could not
have spoken more nobly than that.

Lawrence of Wales

The film that David Lean
    directed in Jordan with Peter
    O'Toole as Lawrence?
                 Lawrence
    was neither golden haired
    nor tall.
        And Lowell Thomas's
    earlier hero-worshipping
    lectures in London that transformed
    Thomas Edward Lawrence
    into Lawrence of Arabia?
                 Vintage
    exploitation at best.
                Lawrence
    was more complex.
              Equally
    adroit with tactics and Arabic,
    he helped the Arabs rout
    the Ottomans.
           Captured in Dar'a,
    where he was tortured and raped,
    he kept the details to himself.
When Lloyd George and Clemenceau
    divided the Middle East
    between them at Versailles,
    he saw his promises betrayed.
Offered a knighthood by the king
    in person, he declined the title
    in the name of justice for the Arabs.
Even when he and Churchill
    offered Faisal and his brother
    a kingdom apiece, it seemed
    inadequate.
          He lived alone
    thereafter, joining the RAF

as Aircraftman Shaw, writing
The Seven Pillars of Wisdom,
and translating Homer into lyrical
English.
         His lone indulgence
was collecting vintage motorcycles.
Speeding on one from his home
  at Clouds Hill, he suffered
    head wounds in a crash and died.
Had he survived, he would
    have had to face the curse
    of fame and unsolicited celebrity.
Reaction to his life and death
    ranged from honor to disdain.
That seems the fate of rebels,
    patriots, and saviors.
                  The public
  has its way with them until
  what's undeniable at last
  prevails and hardens into history.

The Essential Richard Wilbur

Who else but you could make
   a poem pirouette in place
   to its own music?
                         Such art
   can never simply happen
   without the sense of something
   else invoked—some mystery,
   some secret.
                   Call it a miracle
   that guides the hand and heart
   when pen and paper meet.
Call it what mutes analysis
   or calculation.
                 It answers
   to nothing but itself.
                    To be
   accepted and known, it needs
   no more than to be felt
   as love is felt and unforgotten.

The Fate of Some Poets

For the most part, they clump,
   exchange favors, network,
   compete without admitting it,
   and make a tactic of esteem.
Poetry for them is not
   a calling but a fashion.
                  Reciting
   poems in public, they rant
   but rarely rouse.
              Their prosody
   is overblown.
             Their ultimate
   goals are publication, notice,
   and awards.
           Measured against
   mere fame, poor Hopkins was
   a failure.
          Thirty years after
   he died, Robert Bridges
   contrived to have his poems
   published.
          Call it the largesse
   of a British laureate to let
   the poems of a dead man speak
   for themselves ...
          Today how few
   read Bridges?
         How many read Hopkins?

IV
A Fury of Drums

Minimizing Maxims

The light at the end of the tunnel
turns out to be a tiger's eye.

—WISLAWA SZYMBORSKA

An apple a day can be
monotonous.
A bird in hand
has no business there.
Early
to bed and early to rise
assumes you have a choice.
Bards of a feather flock
together.
There's no fool
like an old fool except
an older one.
You're only
young once, and that's the problem.
A fool and his money are
soon parted but sometimes
reunited with interest.
Stench,
a skunk's weapon of choice,
can keep a lion at bay.
Where else can beauty be
but in the eye of the beholder?
Throwing the baby out
with the bathwater isn't funny.
Never judge by appearances
before you look in a mirror.
Anyone who considers honesty
the best policy would be dishonest
if it weren't.

Absence
makes the heart grow.
				More
self-love than love engenders
jealousy, but both make
jealousy possible.
				Beauty
is only skin-deep, but that's
deep enough.
				Hypocrisy
is the price that vice pays
to virtue doubly on Sundays.
The bigger the mouth, the smaller
	the mind.
				Two wrongs don't
make a right, but wars
and executions seem to say
they do.
				If pens are mightier
than swords, why aren't they strong
enough to prove to everyone
that "might makes right" is wrong?

Magnolia in Residence

Magnolias stay in bud
   all winter.
                 Each bud's
   a pen-point long but strong
   enough to weather zero
   and subzero nights.
                Blooming
   in May, the blossoms stay
   pink for more than a month.
Sometimes an unpredicted frost
   will freeze the blossoming magnolia
   by my house, but late in August
   or September, a second blooming
   happens by surprise.
                It's not
   as full or pink as the first
   but just as ready to be noticed.
Then comes December.
                Bracing
   for snow, trees everywhere
   are bare to the bark.
               For one
   magnolia that's outlived
   the drumrolls at Kennedy's funeral,
   the fall of the Soviet Union,
   three wars, and forty-seven Super
   Bowls, what's one more winter?

Overtime

It's much too late to think
   of options or alternatives.
Our Pharaoh-in-Chief is waiting
   like a spoiled prince for loyalists
   to kiss his ring.
                Meanwhile
the little we have saved is taxed
for war.
           No one admits
we've made a hoax of peace
by living behind locked doors
and stashing dollars for the worst.
We're drunk with ultra-security,
   ultra-speed, ultra-vitamins,
   ultra-power.
              We converse
through machines.
               We think
in slogans.
           We worship glitz
and notoriety.
           We choose novels
for "easy reading."
          As for poetry?
It's all reduced to wordplay
   and sociology.
           Meanwhile
the televised and tattooed world
slides by disguised as normal.
We sit and watch.
              Even
when seated, we keep a pistol
holstered at the hip and ready.

We Live with Our Deceptions

September through December
    are numbered out of sequence.
                        Rest-

rooms are not for resting.
To qualify as a founder, one
    of the Founding Fathers fathered
    a foundling.
                The Department of Defense
confirms that war is what
General Smedley Butler
called it ... "a racket."
                    Death
is the common enemy that soldiers
of opposing armies face
together.
             All wars permit
strangers to murder strangers
legally.
           Weak men belittle
women because they fear them.
Women feel what they say
    and do.
           A woman's smile
is her handshake.
                Teresa
of Ávila danced flamenco
in the convent.
                Ordered by the Papal
Nuncio to stop the practice,
Teresa Ali Fatim Corella
Sanchez de Cepeda y Ahumada
slapped him in the face.
                  Four
centuries later she was named

the first female Doctor
of the Church.
                              Newspaper
headlines do not announce
or report the news but inflict it.
Football was "run, tackle
and block" until Rockne
featured the forward pass
to prove that throwing over
was smarter than running through.
Baseball makes time irrelevant
while football and hockey live
and die by the clock.
                              The eyes
of a house are windows that become
polite when curtained.
                              Looking
upward instead of inward
silences the voice of God
within us.
                      For bravery
in public?
                      Jacqueline
Kennedy's four days in November.

What Is Worth Worth?

It starts with drum taps on the rim
   of a snare.
                 A flute whispers
   the opening notes.
                    The tempo
   stays the same but steadily
   intensifies until the ultimate
   crescendo.
                 Signatures change
   as oboes yield to trumpets,
   trumpets to cellos, and cellos
   to saxophones and violins.
Everything ends in a fury
   of drums.
                 The audience stands
   and applauds as for a coronation …
How did a Swiss-Basque Frenchman
   evoke the cadences of Spain
   with such fidelity?
                 Regardless,
   Ravel made light of it,
   saying, "Any conservatory
   student could have done the same."
He ranked it among his lesser
   compositions.
                 Other artists
   have done the same.
                    But why?
Kafka demanded that his writings
   not be published.
                 For Tchaikovsky,
   his *1812 Overture* had
   little merit.
                 Monet destroyed

his water lily paintings by the score
to spite his critics.
                    And Thomas
Aquinas hoped his *Summa
Theologica*, to which he'd given
his life, would be burned "like straw."
What made these four condemn
what millions would cherish?

                         Was it
disgust or simple honesty
that made them trash all judgments
as irrelevant except their own?

By Hand

Seated for dinner, the blind
   man softly touches
   the main course until
   he sees it with his fingers.
                        Later
   he steers a spoonful of corn
   to his mouth without spilling
   a kernel.
             After he drinks,
   he sets the water glass down
   as if it were a chalice on an altar.
The reverence of those who care
   for what they use impresses me.
Painters rinse and dry
   their brushes.
                 Ichiro treasures
   his bats the way a surgeon
   treasures his forceps and scalpels.
Compared to shortcutters
   who send misspelled emails
   or tweets, John Hancock
   wrote his very name as if
   it were a work of art—
   two words with personality.
A doctor's scribbled name
   resembles something he wrote
   with his pen between his toes.
John Hancock's signature
   remains as perfect and everlasting
   now as when he wrote it.

Poetry in Passing

Reviewing your previous poems
  is like revisiting old
  photographs or outgrown clothes.
They're *you* but not quite, not
  now, not lately.
             Whether
  you've outlived them for worse
  or better is irrelevant.
             What's
  recent you prefer because
  they show you've changed the least.
That's not to say they're better.
Poetry scoffs at dates
  and history's other lies.
Wordsworth wrote his best
  before he turned conservative.
His later poems are dismissible.
At sixty, Robinson Jeffers
  never matched the prophecies
  he wrote in his thirties and forties.
Would Keats have faltered
  had he lived past twenty-five?
Housman was over forty
  when he wrote the poems of a lad
  from Shropshire.
             Shakespeare kept
  his syllogistic sonnets flawless
  to the last.
        Antonio Machado
  wrote two lines that many
  Spaniards can recite by heart,
  Caminante, no hay camino,
  se hace el camino al andar.

Translated into English, French,
 or any other language,
 they never lose their force—
 "Wayfarer, there is no road—
 you make the road as you go."
Ben Jonson's sonnet to his son,
 who died at seven, speaks
 for every father since Adam.
Rilke was amazed to say
 his sonnets to Orpheus "arrived
 and imposed themselves" on him.
He wrote them "in a single
 breathless act of obedience."
That's why the sonnets prove
 that only those who've gone
 through hell can make a song
 of pain.
                    And that's why
 literary critics miss
 what only love can grasp.
Perhaps this helps explain
 why Jefferson spent hours
 writing poetry in English,
 Latin, and Greek.
                    After
 Kennedy cited Joyce and Yeats
 in De Valera's presence at the Dail,
 he rallied the echoes of rebellion:
 "We are the boys from Wexford,
 who fought with heart and hand
 to break in twain the galling chain
 and free our native land."
The silence of his audience was truer
 than applause.

But then the ultimate
response is always unexpected.
Asked for the best compliment
he ever received for saying
a poem in public, Laureano
cited one listener's polite
request that he "say it again."

V
From Nowhere
to Nowhere

Venus

Consider Victorine Meurent
   in Manet's *Luncheon on the Grass*.
She seems more naked than nude
   between two well-dressed men
   who stare past her while she
   looks straight at Manet—and us.
The Barcelona whores Picasso
   chose for *Les Demoiselles D'Avignon*
   appear less sensual than awkward.
Clothed or not, Goya's
   Maja looks bored.
                  Pearlstein's
   nudes seem too tired to care ...
But nudity for Venus looks
   permanent by preference ...
The breasts of the girl from Milos
   that Alexandros chose to model
   are sculpted exactly to scale.
Two thousand years later
   in the same Aegean, his sculpture
   was discovered cracked in half
   with both arms missing.
                    Reborn
   complete in polished marble,
   she's draped from the pubis down
   to show her torso upward
   from the hips without a flaw.
Turned a fraction to the left,
   she's stayed at ease alone
   in the Louvre for two centuries
   or more.
            There's not a sign
   of Eve's remorse or any hint
   of Christian shame or guilt.
This lady's nude and unembarrassed.
No one has matched her since.

Oldest Chess Champion Retires at One Hundred

... a look back into the future.

—HANS MAGNUS ENZENSBERGER

To those who hope to live
    in exciting times, I send
    condolences.
                    After excitement,
    what's left but strewn confetti,
    deflated balloons, guttered
    garbage, and windows smashed
    at street level by rocks.
On the higher scale of destruction
    by bomb or shell, consider
    rubbled cities, cemeteries
    groomed like gardens for the fallen
    and, finally, promises that wars
    to end all wars will never
    happen again.
                    What Delmore
    Schwartz called the "scrimmage
    of appetite" survives in different
    forms.
                    Men with initials
    for first names listen and clap
    when money talks.
                            Women
    change faces at fifty to stay
    attractive.
                    Real estate scams
    called skyscrapers multiply
    first floors upward for profit.
Illegibly handwritten names
    on prescriptions and checks are
    never rejected.

                    Meanwhile
everything pretends to be
what it's not so well that nothing's
what it is.
                    When headlines
and the newly but narrowly elected
promise excitement, the generals
salute and choose new wars
to wage but never declare.
It takes cunning, but it works.
In chess the opposite is true.
When nothing's happening,
    everything's ready to happen.
You need the patience of patients
    being patient, of seamstresses
    threading needles at midnight,
    of surgeons slicing a sternum
    to access the heart, of poets
    in mid-poem hoping the words
    will sing.
                    If boredom and time
are demanded, the choice is yours.
Excitement has no future.

Finders, Losers

I've reached a point where time
   is only what passes between
   appointments, dental checkups,
   holidays, and meals.
                     I leave
the distraction of news to those
who need it.
                 I wait as memories,
however dear, just sour
into vague nostalgia.
                      As for
religion?
                 My best friend says
what started as a game between
Greek gods and mortals fractured
into superstition that's become
a business.
               Where does it end?
Is living like a stock-still road
   that keeps on coming and going
   from nowhere to nowhere?
After I lost the one
   I longed to live long with,
   long-life meant nothing more
   than living on.
               Her smiles
were similes for feelings
everyone could share.
                 Her midnight
kisses were truer than thoughts.
I think of coins she kept
   to give away except
   for a rare leftover dime
   she let me find so I
   could buy this poem for her.

Death Benefit

Told that her sickness had
   no cure, the young wife sighed
   and whispered, "Leave it to me
   to take the worst way out."
At fifty-nine Michael announced,
   "No one in my family lived
   longer than sixty."
                    A priest
   defined dialysis as delay,
   deterrence, and debt en route
   to the terminal "d."
               Such quotes
   are pre-obituaries.
                  Facing
   similar fates, a Frenchman
   might favor *joie de vivre.*
Spaniards in song and dance
   recover rapture in grief.
From lost but unforgotten loves
   Arabs create the poetry
   of agony . . .
              Denying death
   is futile as denying gravity,
   but what I seek outlives
   finality.
           All those who think
   of death as rest or sleep
   annoy me.
             If immortality
   is presence forever, what
   could be worse than sleeping
   through it?
          Presences assure us.
Despite our saying that it does,
   the sun never sets.

                                   Beethoven's
            Ninth has no past tense.
        Flamenco dancers trample
            death to dust while clapping.
        After her second heart
            attack, my aunt just laughed.
        But why go on?
                              Facing
            our final firing squads,
            our bravest option is defiance.

                    For Anne Murray Grube

Where in the World?

Not that it's anyone's business,
  but now I'm done with doing
  or having done.
                    I'm out
of challenges, and simply
  keeping busy bores me.
I need to be possessed
  by something unignorable
  as danger or love to make me
act.
        Through similar lulls,
  believers cling to creeds
  that guarantee redemption in advance.
Others pledge themselves to causes
  or kings whose sole demands
  are loyalty and silence.
                  Some age
  in affluent ease and die
  from decay.
         Today I listen
  to a grafted wild cherry I planted
  in the yard for Mary Anne.
It grew like a double-tree
  forking from a single trunk.
Her side *flowered* while mine
  just *leafed* ...
            Both spoke the wisdom
  of wild cherries rooted in place ...
The longer I watch, the more
  I'm certain it's wiser to *be*
  than to *do*.
          Like poetry and prose
  emerging from a single seed,
  this marriage of flowers and leaves
  stays totally itself and waits
  for nothing more than to be seen.

Written Off

They don't teach handwriting anymore. They say we don't need it.

—MY GRANDSON

———————————————

John Donne confessed: "I cannot
   say I loved, for who can say
   he was killed yesterday?"
                            Anyone
   who ever loved agrees.
                           Equally
   ironic was Minucius Felix:
   "Is it not foolish to worship
   what one ought to weep for,
   and to weep for what one ought
   to worship?"
                  That's dated tomorrow.
Robert Frost insisted that
   the sound of words should match
   their sense, which makes speed-
   reading an insult to poetry
   and a total waste of attention.
Flaubert dismissed all progress
   as vain unless it was moral.
Immoral progress still prevails.
All these are quotes from books
   I've read.
                Quoting or jotting
   notes in margins or underlining
   words is how I chat
   with authors as I read.
                       It lifts
   communication to communion.
Screen viewing fails because it
   seems more public than a reader's
   privacy before a page.

Viewing's gift is recognition.
Understanding comes with words.
That's why I'm close to books
  in all their bound variety—
  the bookness of books.

                          And yet
  what else are books but scripts
  translated into print?

                      Each written
  page produces multiple printed
  copies, affirming the root
  difference between machinofacturing
  and manufacturing—made by hand.
The privacy I taste while reading
  handwritten letters is even
  more intimate.

                        The writer's
  presence on the page is life
  itself transcribed.

                        Why else
  are letters of love, praise,
  gratitude, or understanding rarely
  thrown away?

                    What the heart
  prompts the hand to say
  on paper has no equal.

                        Imagine
  discovering a handwritten sonnet
  of Shakespeare's signed by Shakespeare.
Imagine it side by side
  with thousands of printed copies
  of the same sonnet.

                      Which one
  seems the truer?

                    Which one
  brings you closer to Shakespeare?

O Say Can't You See?

We shout when we should be discussing,
   and the country in chaos accepts it.
We shoot when we should be disarming,
   and the country in chaos accepts it.
We claim that the poor are just lazy,
   and the country in chaos accepts it.
We budget to build bigger prisons,
   and the country in chaos accepts it.
We blunder in wars that are endless,
   and the country in chaos accepts it.
We lie and deny that we're lying,
   and the country in chaos accepts it.
We bicker like lawyers for peanuts,
   and the country in chaos accepts it.
We covet the fame of the famous,
   and the country in chaos accepts it.
We say without money we're nothing,
   and the country in chaos accepts it.

The country in chaos accepts it
   when churches are run by accountants.
The country in chaos accepts it
   when teachers are mocked if they picket.
The country in chaos accepts it
   when oldsters are warehoused to wither.
The country in chaos accepts it
   when snipers are honored for murders.
The country in chaos accepts it
   when leaders see voters as suckers.
The country in chaos denies it
   when phone calls are tapped and recorded.
The country in chaos denies it
   when hucksters control the elections.
The country in chaos denies it
   when mothers are torn from their children.

The country in chaos denies it
    when what we call learning is training.

When artists are silenced as traitors,
    the country in chaos denies it.
When nobody speaks for the needy,
    the country in chaos denies it.
When murders are common as muggings,
    the country in chaos denies it.
When nothing else matters but winning,
    the country in chaos denies it.
When losers are said to deserve it,
    the country in chaos denies it.
When tattoos exist for the gawkers,
    the country in chaos denies it.
When sex is just something to market,
    the country in chaos denies it.
When only the chosen are favored,
    the country in chaos denies it.
When a country's already in chaos,
    what good does it do to deny it?

VI
The Birthmarks
of Pain

A Loner Breaks His Silence

God is the last refuge of loners.

—MARGUERITE YOURCENAR

What else is left?
　　　　　Without love,
　desire's a tyrant.
　　　　　Without desire,
　whatever's Platonic offers
　nothing but thought, just thought.
The myths of romance cannot
　replace the Once, Only,
　and Always.
　　　　　Result?
　　　　　　The curse
　of brevity defines each life
　as tragically mortal.
　　　　　The same
　is true of beauty.
　　　　　Jasmine,
　asphodel, and orchids bloom
　their way to rot.
　　　　　It seems
　that nothing saddens sooner
　than attainment.
　　　　　Some say
　that fame's the one exception.
Spare me the sight of medals
　in their velvet boxes, coins
　and stamps minted with profiles,
　honorific robes and photos

of crowds clapping and smiling
like beauty contest finalists.
Acclaim insults significance.
The last recourse is God,
    who answers silence with silence.

What Time Is It?

"Our present," stated the poet,
   "is the future past."
                    He meant
   that every day in his country
   was yesterday forever.
                    Yesterday's
   halfbacks sound the same
   when they recount important
   touchdowns only they recall.
And so do many women
   sipping coffee and thinking
   how beautiful they once were
   without makeup.
                    They smile
   non-smiles, remembering.
                    You
   never see veterans of combat
   smile like that.
                  Or cancer survivors.
Or tourists who checked in
   too late to be aboard
   the flight that crashed.
                  For them
   what else is there to say?
Each time you visit neighborhoods
   unchanged as cemeteries or meet
   old classmates from decades back
   who have to say they're who
   they are, the world of right now
   disappears.
                  You can smile
  or not.
                  It makes no difference.

A Tale of Two Ankles

1

The left one cracked on ice.
Seeing it askew, I tried
   to right it, but the crack
   was undeniable.
                          Results?
Paramedics, ambulance, X-rays,
   surgery, and then a knee-high
   cast that slept with me
   for weeks.
                  The right-footed
driver I became did well
   enough, but crutches were
   my bane.
                   Stripped of the cast,
I flexed my toes, did daily
   knee-bends, and strode in place
   until my leg was mine
   again ...
               The right one broke
on the stairs without a sound.
What followed was familiar:
   X-rays, splints, ice bags
   to lessen swelling, surgical
   screws and a plate.
                   Tonight
   my leg is helplessly itself.
Its future is ibuprofen,
   rest, and rehabilitation.
                  Cracking
   the left ankle made me regret
   the trips I had to cancel
   and promises I had to break.
Breaking the right one has made
   me indifferent to that.

       Why fret
 about travel, visits, and the rest
 if all that matters is within?
I choose to learn the patience
 of expectant mothers in late
 pregnancy.
      They know that life
 and growing are the same,
 but waiting is the price.
        Last
 night I read a paragraph
 by Marguerite Yourcenar.
         She found
 aggressive feminism incomplete
 because it never stressed
 those challenges that men ignore
 but women live to overcome.
"Equality is not identity."
Today I'm learning as I heal
 exactly what she meant by that.

      2

Compared to turnarounds
 from transplant surgery, serious
 strokes or amputation, it ranks
 quite low.
       Bone-time's over
 in weeks or months, but slowly,
 slowly.
     The days repeat
 themselves with different names.
Braced and bandaged, I make
 my peace with pain like someone
 sentenced to life on life's terms.
I'm told that broken bones

can heal stronger than they were
before.

    I'm told, I'm told ...
Again I think of women
 in the third trimester.

        Their only
option is to wait.

      Compliance
is assumed.

     Endurance is required
on demand.

     Annoyance is irrelevant.

Before the Pen Runs Dry

Each time we write to learn
   how much we think we know,
   we stand convicted of our own
   timidity.
            Aging, we look
   subdued as penitents waiting
   to be told how far they've fallen
   from the norm of "total wellness."
After we choose to damn
   those lies that bracket life
   with long-living—or happiness
   with plenty—or wealth with worth,
   we opt for loving those
   we cherish most and doing
   what we love to do.
            Compared
   with these, the Sunday reflex
   called religion seems hollow
   as posthumous living upgraded
   as "assisted."
            So does our wont
   to deify or nickname generals
   or sanction art, poetry, music,
   and theater only if they're "non-
   controversial."
            Why not concede
   such folly to amnesia and admit
   that time matters least when love
   matters most?
            Carping on a sheet
   of paper with a pen solves nothing.
What outlives history is all
   we have.

"I Am Who Am"
is God defined by God.
What's lost if we attempt
to live the same and let
the past and future vanish
like the total frauds they are?

In the Red

If memory means losing track
   of time, I more than qualify.
Was Kennedy murdered yesterday
   or fifty-six Novembers ago?
Were my grandchildren just born,
   or are they really twenty,
   seventeen, and twelve?
                        The maple
   I replanted can't be higher
   than my roof already, but it is.
I still recall my rifle
   number but forget (or want
   to forget) who's President.
Don't talk to me about
   inflation, taxes, or weekends
   at Disney World.
                      Nothing's
   contemporary very long.
I've lost count of birthdays.
I stumble on stairs I climbed
   two at a time last year.
Today I pulled off the road
   to be sure I knew where
   I was going ...
                For reassurance
   I glance at a branch of my maple
   where a male and female cardinal
   are perched at attention.
                    Paired
   for life, they look as if
   they've found what everybody seeks.
He's royally red and poised

like the god of love invoked
by worshippers.
                    She looks less vivid
but seems more sensible and smarter.

                    For Shea Murtaugh

Waiting Means Knowing When Not To

I'd spent two weeks rejecting
    what was not worth writing.
The subjects were there—thousands,
    millions of subjects—but none
    gave wings to words.
                         If I
had forced myself to write
something earthbound but merely
correct, it would have seemed
like dancing without music.
                              I opted

for silence.
              The world and I
were still at odds until
I thought of how a nurse
reacted to a story I shared ...
Two brothers had married
    two sisters, one of whom
    could conceive but not bear
    a child.
              Her sister volunteered
to bear the baby for her
and did.
              Years later, a friend
asked her how it felt to be
a "surrogate mother."
                  "Look,"
answered the sister, who was
then the mother of five sons,
"I offered room and board for nine
months, and my sister would
have done the same for me."
The nurse smiled and said,

"I did the same thing last year for my cousin ... in exchange for nine months you give somebody a lifetime ... if you have time to do it, why not?"

Last Words Last

Farewells eviscerate because
    they are the words that last.
They're treacherous as poems that way.
They share the merciless birthmarks
    of pain.
            Authors would claim
they said the words.
                 In fact
the words said them.
                   Some
were final as Hamlet's after
he was stabbed, "I am dead,
Horatio."
            Or Joe DiMaggio's,
"I'll finally get to see
Marilyn again."
            Or Angelo
Roncalli's whisper to his doctor,
Ho fatto le valige, e sono
pronto a partire.
               While spending
my last minutes with Mary Anne,
I searched for words like these
before eternity broke in.

VII
Forever Has
No Dates

In Troth

Forget the birthdays.
For me
you're younger than ever.
Nothing
is truer than that.
Tonight
I thought of life without you,
and I died—no one to kid
or kiss, no one to say
that blue is not my color,
no one to shuck mussels with
from the same bowl, no one
to live the patience that is love
in waiting.
You're always new
to know—a mate I choose
all over every day.
You make
our lives seem one long day
with no past tense.
I love you
for the times you've slowed me down
before I would have blundered.
I love you for the hundred ways
you saw what I would
never see until you'd seen it
first.
We're nip and tuck,
saddle and boot, a pair
of gloves, a study in rhyme
from A to Z without a flub
between.
We're grateful so
for one lone son whose music
loops the globe, grandchildren

three, and Dawn who keeps
all five in love together
and intact.
                    If I could make
right now eternal as a song,
I would.
                    Impossible, of course.
But not the wanting to ...
                                        That's why
I want impossibility to last,
regardless.
                    That's happiness.

Nightly

I wake each day to face
   the tyranny of certainties
   that rhyme with age.
                         Next come
   the obstinate laws of science
   where life is only what
   I taste, touch, see, hear, or smell
   as well as what I name
   in passing with the curse of words.
For some who look for more,
   there's always the mythology
   of God's parting the Red Sea
   or Christ's walking on the waves
   in Galilee.
                  As for the righteous
   who assume that miracles will spare
   them everything they fear?
I leave them to their dreams ...
I trust in love ongoing
   from time present into presence.
I'm grateful for seven hundred
   and fifty-three months we shared
   and share still, share now.
                        You
   made a poem out of each day's
   prose.
          To live that life
   again for one more day
   with you, I'd swap the world.

One Night at a Time

You kept the outcome at a distance
   with your smile, but the end
   was scripted in advance.
                             Each time
   our eyes locked, the tears
   came.
              I had to turn away.
You held my hand—the left.
Each night in what passes
   now for sleep, I wake
   to learn how absence crucifies.
What can I do to give
   this grief an ounce of dignity?
Nothing compares with it.
Only the ache of not having
   you beside me brings you
   back and keeps you close.

Stages

Lose parents, and you lose the past. Lose children, and you lose the future. Lose your mate, and you lose the present.

—AN ADAGE

Without having you to care
    or care for, I'm helpless
    as a driver of a car sliding
    sideways downhill on ice.
I've lost my taste for all
    enjoyment.
                Some say diversion
    is the answer.
                I say diversion
    is distraction, nothing more.
Others say I should be
    grateful for the years we shared.
I say I am, I *am*,
    but what I feel is truer
    than words or years.
                Because
    forever has no dates, I'm
    jealous of eternity and God.

One More Year, One Year Less

Without you I am sentenced
    to myself.
              The house we chose
together has a past that's always
present: Waterford glasses
you treasured, sunflowers
you brought from Cannes and vased,
the sculpture Starchev gave you
after you praised it.
                  They help me
feel you're near.
             In photographs
you smile as my bride, my wife,
and later as a mother hugging
three grandchildren on our sixtieth.
Never forced or false, your smile
was everywhere and always
you.
         Each day for more
than sixty years that smile
saved me.
             And saves me still.

God's Gift to Me

My dearest Mary Anne,
    I'm no more reconciled
    than I was three months ago.
You're everywhere I look—
    from raincoats hangered
    in a closet to framed photographs
    to car keys for a car
    you never drove.
                I sleep
and wake now on your side
of the bed ...
            To say that other
men have lost their wives
is no relief.
            Devastation
stays particular and merciless
if shared or not.
            Longevity
offers nothing but more
of the same or worse ...
                I miss
your face, your voice, your calm
defiance in your final months,
your last six words that will be
mine alone forever.
              Darling,
you were my life as surely
as you are my life today
and will be always.
              We're close
as ever now but differently.
"Why do we have to die?"
you asked.

I had no answer.
My answer now is rage
and tears that sentence death
to death each day I wake
without but always with you.

One Another's Best

It happens when what I say
   and what I'd hoped to say
   are one and the same, and even
   better than I hoped.
                  The sure
   perfection of it lingers.
Gratitude seems not enough.
I want to let the world
   know, but quietly—so quietly
   that no one hears me but
   myself.
            It's like discovering
   love for the first, last,
   and only time.
             The once
   of it gladdens but saddens.
"Sorrow ends," wrote Shakespeare,
   "not when it seemeth done."
My only one, my dearest,
   your requiem and birthday
   happened together.
             Was this
   your way or God's of promising
   that right now and forever
   would someday be the same
   for us, regardless of the odds?

The Renegade

As for life after death?
Many
believe, but no one really
knows.
All those who claim
they know equate belief
with knowledge for psychiatric,
not spiritual reasons.
They
find living with uncertainty
impossible.
Believers pray
in gratitude, but doubts persist
even with the most devout.
They want to take Christ's words
as scrivened by his four
stenographers and say amen.
Death is the problem—the fact
of death.
Reactions range
from fear to love.
The fearful
die living.
But always when those
most loved are taken, lovers
discover that love buries death.
The dead survive as presences
in dreams or thoughts that mock
whatever passes for resting
in peace.
After thirty-three
years of breath and three days
of death, the Messiah rose
to resume living with those
He loved.

                    Compared with that,
who needs theology or ritual
for reassurance?
                              What's truer for God
or each of us than unions
resurrected as reunions?
                                   What else
is faith but trusting that loves
once known will be known forever?

Credits

Some of these poems have appeared in *Undocumented*; *Great Lakes Anthology: Poets on Social Justice*; *What Saves Us: Poems of Empathy and Outrage in the Age of Triumph*; *Modern Age*; *Notre Dame Magazine*; *Fifth Wednesday Journal*; *Literary Matters*; *Angelus*; *Pittsburgh Post-Gazette*; *Pittsburgh Quarterly*; *Salmagunds*; and *Yale Review*.

Samuel Hazo

The author of books of poetry, fiction, essays, and plays, Samuel Hazo is the founder and director of the International Poetry Forum in Pittsburgh, Pennsylvania. He is also the McAnulty Distinguished Professor of English Emeritus at Duquesne University, where he taught for forty-three years. From 1950 until 1957, he served in the US Marine Corps, completing his tour as a captain. He earned a bachelor of arts degree, magna cum laude, from the University of Notre Dame, a master of arts degree from Duquesne University, and a doctorate from the University of Pittsburgh. His previous works include *And the Time Is, They Rule the World, Like a Man Gone Mad*, and *Sexes: The Marriage Dialogues* (poetry); *The Time Remaining* and *This Part of the World* (fiction); *Watching Fire, Watching Rain*, and *Tell It to the Marines* (drama); *The Stroke of a Pen* and *Outspokenly Yours* (essays); *Smithereened Apart* (critique of the poetry of Hart Crane); *The Pittsburgh That Stays within You* (memoir awarded the 2018 IPPY national bronze citation for creative nonfiction); and *The World within the Word: Maritain and the Poet* (critique). His translations include Denis de Rougemont's *The Growl of Deeper Waters*, Nadia Tueni's *Lebanon: Twenty Poems for One Love*, and Adonis's *The Pages of Day and Night*. In 2003, a selective collection of his poems, *Just Once*, received the Maurice English Poetry Award. Hazo has been awarded twelve honorary doctorates. He was honored with the Griffin Award for Creative Writing from the University of Notre Dame, his alma mater, and was chosen to receive his tenth honorary doctorate from the university in 2008. A National Book Award finalist, he was named Pennsylvania's first state poet by Governor Robert Casey in 1993, and he served until 2003.

When Not Yet Is Now was designed in Meta Serif Pro, with Impact and Meta Pro display type, and composed by Kachergis Book Design of Pittsboro, North Carolina. It was printed on 60-pound Maple Eggshell Cream and bound by Maple Press of York, Pennsylvania.